Dear Laura

THE LITTLE HOUSE BOOKS

By Laura Ingalls Wilder

Illustrated by Garth Williams

LITTLE HOUSE IN THE BIG WOODS

LITTLE HOUSE ON THE PRAIRIE

FARMER BOY

ON THE BANKS OF PLUM CREEK

BY THE SHORES OF SILVER LAKE

THE LONG WINTER

LITTLE TOWN ON THE PRAIRIE

THESE HAPPY GOLDEN YEARS

THE FIRST FOUR YEARS

LITTLE HOUSE
Laura Ingalls Wilder

Dear Laura

LETTERS FROM CHILDREN TO

Laura Ingalls Wilder

HarperCollins*Publishers*

We gratefully acknowledge the Laura Ingalls Wilder–Rose Wilder Lane Home Association in Mansfield, Missouri, and the Herbert Hoover Library in West Branch, Iowa, for granting us access to their archives of children's letters to Laura Ingalls Wilder. All photographs are courtesy of the Laura Ingalls Wilder–Rose Wilder Lane Home Association unless otherwise indicated. We have made our best efforts to locate the writers of these letters to Laura Ingalls Wilder, but in many cases our efforts have been unsuccessful. If any reader can tell us where any of the writers can be found, we would be grateful.

HarperCollins®, ■®, Little House® are trademarks of HarperCollins Publishers Inc.

Dear Laura
Letters from Children to Laura Ingalls Wilder
Copyright © 1996 by HarperCollins Publishers, Inc.

Library of Congress Cataloging-in-Publication Data
Dear Laura : letters from children to Laura Ingalls Wilder.
    p.   cm. — (Little house)
    Summary: A collection of children's letters from the 1930s through the 1950s sent to Laura Ingalls Wilder, author of the nine Little House books.
    ISBN 0-06-026275-3 (lib. bdg.). — ISBN 0-06-026274-5
    1. Wilder, Laura Ingalls, 1867–1957—Correspondence.   2. Women authors, American—20th century—Correspondence.   3. Children—United States—Correspondence.   4. Children—Books and reading.
[1. Wilder, Laura Ingalls, 1867–1957—Correspondence.   2. Children's writings.   3. Books and reading.]
I. Wilder, Laura Ingalls, 1867–1957.   II. Series.]
PS3545.I342Z48 1996   95–9708
813'.52—dc20   CIP
                                                                                          AC

Typography by Alicia Mikles
1 2 3 4 5 6 7 8 9 10
❖
First Edition

Children have loved the Little House books by Laura Ingalls Wilder ever since they were first published in the 1930's. Laura once said that she wrote the books because "I wanted children now to understand what is behind the things they see, what it is that made America the way they know it." And children responded to Laura's stories of the frontier with so much enthusiasm that many of them wrote to tell her how much they enjoyed her books and how much they loved her for writing them. Almost immediately after the publication of *Little House in the Big Woods* in 1932 and until her death in 1957, Laura received hundreds and hundreds of fan letters from children. Children of all ages wrote, and boys and girls alike wrote to Laura at her home on Rocky Ridge Farm in Mansfield, Missouri. They wrote from every state in the country—from suburban houses, farms, apartment buildings, hospitals, and school classrooms. But no matter what their age was, or where they wrote from, all the children who wrote to Laura thought of her as a close and much-loved friend. In fact, many of the children called her by her first name, just as if she were someone they had always known.

What exactly did these children share with Laura in their letters? Many of them asked the same questions: Is the Laura who wrote the books the same person as the Laura in the books? What happened to Mary, Carrie, and Grace, and all the other people Laura mentions in the Little House books? Some children told Laura about their favorite Little House chapter, and some told her about their own school days and houses. Some of the letters were written during World War II, and these letters speak of brothers who are in the army, and of gas rations that prevented a longed-for vacation. And almost every single letter asks Laura to write more books and to continue the story of her life with Almanzo.

The children also sent Laura beautiful birthday and Valentine's Day cards they had made for her. They sent her poems they had written, and photographs of themselves, their families, or their school classes. They sent her pictures they had drawn of scenes from the Little House books. One school class even sent Laura an autograph album with a greeting and signature on every page from a different student!

Laura was as devoted to her young fans as they were to her. Until the rheumatism in her hands made it too painful for her to write, Laura answered every letter by hand. She would write notes in pencil on the back of the envelope to remind herself what questions she needed to answer in her reply. Laura's replies were sometimes the very first letters some of the children had ever received, and often these children would write back to thank her— and Laura would reply again. Even when she was not able to answer her fan mail herself, Laura saved every letter, often in its original envelope.

It is because Laura herself saved all her fan letters that this book exists today. Over 100 of the most delightful, entertaining, and heartwarming letters by the very first children to read and love the Little House books have been gathered together for this collection. The spelling, grammar, and punctuation have been almost entirely preserved, so that these letters are just as Laura herself would have seen them. Included in this collection are more than 30 facsimiles of actual letters, as well as many reproductions of the wonderful drawings, photographs, gifts, valentines, and cards that Laura received. These letters and cards came from the hearts of Laura's most adoring fans, who had grown to know and love her so well in her Little House books that they wanted to share a bit of their lives with her, just as she had shared hers with them.

Laura Ingalls Wilder, around 1917

August 16, 1932

Dear Miss Wilder,

    Mother and I have just finished The Little House in the Big Woods. I loved that story and I want you to write some more books like that. I am seven years old and I am in the Second Grade.

                    Your little friend,
                    Evelyn
                    Colebrook, Conn.

January 3, 1933

Dear Mrs. Wilder,

    I am a little girl in the fifth grade. We are studying about books and Authors. Each of us has chosen an author we like and is trying to find out all we can about them. I love your "Little House in the Big Woods." Will you please tell me some thing about your self?
    I will be so happy to hear from you.

                    Your friend,
                    Mary Ruth
                    Concord, N.C.

May 8, 1934

Dear Mrs. Wilder,

   I am one of the very fortunate children to have read your excellent book, "Little House In the Big Woods." The part that interested me most was when Laura and Mary were going to town. It seemed very strange that the children would think it a great honor to go to town. The reason my class enjoyed hearing your book was because it was particularly about your childhood. Thank you for writing your lovely book. We would be very glad to have a reply from you.

                              Sincerely yours,
                              Helen
                              Fifth Grade, Fulton School
                              Mount Vernon, N.Y.

Minneapolis Minn.
June 3, 1937

Ɖ Mrs. Wilder,
Our teacher read the two
books that you wrote.
I love them.
I want to know if Jack hurt
himself and do you wish
you were a little girl again
with your Ma and Pa. I hope
you like our posters and I
wish you a happy vacation.
Your friend, Lee Thomas.

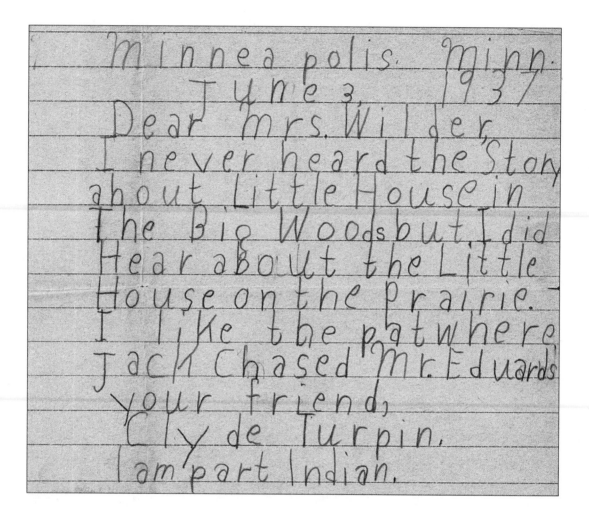

Minneapolis. Minn.
June 3, 1937
Dear Mrs. Wilder,
I never heard the Story
about Little House in
The Big Woods but, I did
Hear about the Little
House on the Prairie.
I like the pat where
Jack Chased Mr. Eduards
Your friend,
Clyde Turpin.
I am part Indian.

February 5, 1941

Dear Mrs. Wilder,

Our room has been reading your books. I have
enjoyed them very much. My Grandmother lived when
you did. Do you remember the Grasshopper Weather?
My Grandmother said she remembers it, but she lived in
Missouri by the Missisippi River. Some of the boys and
girls have asked you for your picture. I would have asked
you about Mary and Carrie but some of the boys and
girls have already. I would like it too. I am a twin and we
take books home and my sister reads them to me. Your
Pa was very kind, wasn't he? Please tell us all about yourself. I hope you have a Happy Valentine's Day.

Sincerely yours,
Jeannine
Lansing, Mich.

July 24, 1941

Dear Mrs. Wilder,

I am writing in behalf of a little girl who adores your books. My grandniece, Mary Jane (now eleven), loves your stories above any she has read. I know that they have so entered into her life that, if she lives to be an old lady, "Laura" and her family will always be flesh-and-blood friends of hers. Recently Mary Jane's mother said that more than any other gift Mary Jane would love to have a complete set of your books. So I am planning to bring that about.

Would you be so kind as to send an inscription which I could insert in one of the volumes I shall buy? Mary Jane would be pleased beyond words and so would all her family.

With my gratitude and best wishes to you I am

Sincerely yours,
Clara
Englewood, N.J.

Dear Mary Jane Hunt,

   It makes me very happy that you love Pa and Ma and the girls, so here is my wish for you, —

May your life be long and happy.

May your friends be gay and true.

May the joy of love and laughter, Ever hover over you

                    Your friend
                    Laura Ingalls Wilder
     L.
     Laura of the stories

This is the letter Laura sent to Clara to give to her grandniece, Mary Jane.

3030 Parker,
Dearborn Mich,
Oct. 9, 1941

Dear Mrs. Wilder,

I am a girl from the Oxford School. Beverly Wirth read us a letter she had received from you.

I've read quite a few of your books and like them very much. I like them because your characters are so real and they act just like other boys and girls

I am sorry to hear that your sister Mary died. I like and remember Mary so well because she wanted to be a teacher and I would like to be one too.

I am glad to hear you are writing a new book and I'm ~~glad~~ anxious

2.

to read it and find
out if Mary went to
college and became a
teacher.

The last book I
read was "Long Winter."
I feel sorry for Pa and
Laura (you) who had to
sit in the woodshed and
twist haysticks.

When I think of
poor Grace who had hardly
any Christmas I will be
thankful of the things
I recieve.

I'm thankful you
wrote those books for
girls and boys like me to
read.

Very Sincerely Yours,
Mary L. Jones

Mary Louise Jones
3030 Parker,
Dearborn Michigan.

November 3, 1941

Dear Mrs. Wilder,

   I like your books. We are on the second book. It is
"On The Banks Of Plum Creek." It is real good. Laura
is always getting into something.

   I hope you will be able to come to see us. I would
like to see you very much. Try to come and visit our
school.

   In our room we have, a fish bowl. We have five fish.
And we have three snails. We enjoy them a lots.

                              Sincerely,
                              Jacquelyn
                              Anne E. West School
                              Atlanta, Ga.

804 Essie Ave S.E.
Atlanta Ga.
Nov 8, 1941

Dear Mrs Wilder,

I thought it very good when Anna Nelson got Charlotte, your rag doll. When I was only nine years old, I had a doll named Sugar Pie. One day a dog got her but I got her back. She was in the dog's house. All the books we have read were very good and I have enjoyed them very much.

Sincerely yours,
Barbara Sue Harper.

November 6, 1941

My Dear Mrs. Wilder,

My teacher has been reading your books to our Fourth Grade at De Veaux School in Toledo Ohio. I have enjoyed them so much that I wish to own the set, so that I may read them over many times. I am earning the money to buy them. I have almost enough to buy "The Little House in the Big Woods."

This week is book week. Our room is going to tell stories from different chapters in three of your books in the auditorium.

Our Librarian told us that you have written a new book. I am glad, and hope you will write us many more.

Very sincerely,
David
Toledo, Ohio

November 25, 1941

Dear Mrs. Wilder,

I have read some of your books, they were very nice. They were Little House in the Big Woods, Little House on the Prairie, and On the Banks of Plum Creek. We are in the middle of On the Banks of Plum Creek. I will send you a picture of me and my sister. It was taken at Christmas. If you will send me a picture of you when you were a little girl and one like you are now. I would like your autograph on both of your picture. Please wright and tell me the name of your books that our class hasnot read. I am in the Fourth Grade. The only thing that I want for Christmas is the four books named, Little House in the Big Woods, Little House on the Prairie, and On the Banks of Plum Creek and your picture. Please come and see me. I would love to see you. Please bring your husband to.

Sincerely Yours,
Susan
Toledo, Ohio

November 28, 1941

Dear Mrs. Wilder,

I am a girl of nine. I am writing you about your lovely books. I love them very much and was very happy when the new one was publised. As soon as I have gotten one of your books I read it trough as slowly as I can such as one chaper every day but I never can do that little because I enjoy them very much. As soon as I have finished the book I always let Nancy, a friend of mine borrow it. I now have these books

Little House in the Big Woods

Little House on the Prairie

On the Banks of Plum Creek

On the Shores of Silver Lake

The Long Winter

Little Town on the Prairie

I know you have written one called Farmer Boy but I havent gotten it yet since it is not one about you.

Was Nellie Oleson really so bad? Did Mary Love college?

I have a large bookcase of books but yours are much my favorites.

All the books you have written when put together are seven. I read on the flap of one that there were to be only seven. Nancy and I are hopeing there will be more. Pease, please write another or two.

Nancy and I made dress up dresses. Mine is pink percale with white flowers. It has a long full skirt, buttons at back and puff sleeves. Nancy's is the same except its a blueish green print on white ground. I have a pink bonnet and one petticoat. I hope to make another soon. I have 2 hoops which we wear to help hold them out as Nancy has no petticoats and I have only one.

I have a playhouse which is large, has a fire place and old fashiond furniture. I am much more interested in your books than I think most girls would be.

Sorry to bother you!

Loveingly,
Blakeley
Gloucester, Mass.

P.S. Please excuse bad writeing and spelling.

November 30, 1941

Dear Mrs. Wilder,

I could not wait till christmas to read Little Town on The Prairie. I love it even more than your others. Nellie olson is such a funny name. Are Carrie, Grace and Mary still living? when will you write another book? please tell more about you and Almanzo.

Love,
John
Media, Penn.

Mrs. A. J. Wilder.
Rocky Ridge Farm.
Mansfield,
missouri.

January 2, 1942

Dear Mrs. Wilder,

This Christmas I received your new book "Little Town On the Prairie." I finished the day after Christmas, and have just finished it a 2nd time. It is very good.

I have just finished telling my mother how the proposed paper shortage may cut out the publication of your books, and how we ought to get the rest of the books you have written. She looked as if the idea was good, and maybe—

One of the boys in my class, Cammie, has all your books, and he lent them to our school library, so I have read them.

The minute I received my present of your book, I sat down to start it. But my aunt, (she is sort of cross) said "No, wait until we are finished." So I had to growl to my self and wait.

In reading I came across Nellie Olsen again. What became of her? And also Royal Wilder? Mary Power and Minnie are to other questions? Can you answer them?

Sincerely yours,
Rebecca
George School
Newtown, Penn.

January 2, 1942

Dear Laura Ingalls Wilder,

It may seem strange to get a letter from somebody you don't know but here it is anyway. Your books are the best books I have ever read. I mean it too. I am eleven now. I was six when I got Little House in the Big Woods. Now I have the whole set.

I wish you would write another book. As soon as I hear that another book is coming out I tell mother and she gets it for me. When ever I find somebody who has not read your books I lend them my books. I have not found anybody who doesn't like them. What makes me like them still better is knowing that they are true. I like books best about that time. I live out in the country but I wish I lived on a farm. I am like your husband Almanzo. I love horses. When I grow up I hope to be a doctor.

Love,
Ursula
Moylan, Penn.

P.S. This year I had a very Merry Christmas and Happy New Year

I

LOVE YOU

you will never be able to tell who this is from so I will tell you
Ursula W. Brown

Roses are Red Violets are Bule Sugar is sweet and so are you Please Be my Valentine

January 3, 1942

Dear Laura,

    I like your books a lot.

    My mother has read them all to me because I am just seven years old. I would like it if you would write some more books. We want to hear about Almanzo and the sleigh ride and your schoolteaching and Mary and her coming home and you marrying Almanzo and other things. Please write one in time for next Christmas.

                        Lots of love,
                        Anne
                        Chapel Hill, N.C.

January 12, 1942

Dear Mrs. Wilder,

I feel like I know you well, because I have all your books, and have read them all many, many times.

Each Christmas, when you have a new book out, my mother and Dad give me the book. I am fourteen, my brother sixteen, and my sister is eleven, but just the same, we all enjoy the book as much as anyone, as do Mother and Dad.

Ever since we have gotten the books, Dad has read them out loud to us, winter evenings, because then the whole family can enjoy it, together.

Every Christmas, since we have been able to read, our parents have given us at least one book a piece. By now, we have all built up a large library of our own.

My brother, sister and I have always loved reading. Before we could read, mother and dad read to us every evening, so we could hardly wait to go to school, so we could read the books to ourselves.

I won't keep you any longer; but I would love, if you're not too busy, to get a letter from you, answering some of the questions in my mind . . . . . . are Carrie, Grace or Mary still alive?

And thank you for all the family pleasure you have brought us.

Sincerely,
Jane
Pasco, Wash.

February 12, 1942

Dear Mrs. Wilder,

Our childrens librarian told us that you were having a birthday this month so I am writing to wish you a very happy birthday.

I am reading one of your books. The name of it is "By the Shores of Silver Lake." You must have had a very interesting life to have written such interesting books.

Our teacher is Mrs. Brooks. At present our main subject is Geography. We are studying Spanish also.

We have four teams in the sixth grade. Each team is trying to get more words than the other one.

At one-thirty every afternoon someone reads some book to us. Miss Crawford usually sends us a book from the city Library.

We are selling Defense Stamps and Bonds at our school. We have sold over $350.00 worth already.

I hope you have many more very happy birthdays and get many valentines.

Your friend,
Beverly
Lowell School
Winfield, Kans.

February 13, 1942

Dear Mrs. Wilder,

I have read most of your books and have enjoyed
them very much. The ones I haven't read are never in.
Everyone else must like them too.

My girl friend must be very proud to have her birthday
in the same month as yours.

Mrs. Brooks suggested we start studying Spanish
words. All of us like to get new words. We have words
such as "Adios" meaning good bye and "Buenos dias"
as good morning.

If you know any words, we would appreciate it very
much if you could give us some.

I must close now.

Very Sincerely,
Beverly
Lowell School
Winfield, Kans.

February 20, 1942

Dear Mrs. Wilder,

In English we have been studying about Our Nation's Heroes whose birthdays are in February. We learned that <u>your</u> birthday is sometime in February. We think of you as our friend. We want to wish you a <u>very</u> happy birthday and lots and lots of them.

Your sincere friends,
The fourth grade girls,
Webster School
Winfield, Kans.

February 20, 1942

Dear Mrs. Wilder,

Happy Birthday Mrs. Wilder! I have read many of your books. The one I liked best was "Little House on the Prairie." I live on a farm and have a Shepherd puppy. I hope you have many happy birthdays after this one.

Sincerely yours,
Verdeen Louise
Fifth grade
Winfield, Kans.

February 23, 1942

Dear Laura Ingalls Wilder,

I am a Junior High School student. I'll be fourteen in June.

I have read your books ever since early grade school days. I am taking this opportunity to tell you how much your books have meant to mother and me. We have just finished reading one of your latest books titled "Little Town on the Prairie." Needless to say we are anxiously awaiting for another of your interesting and inspiring books. Will there be one soon?

Would I be impertinent in asking for a small autographed picture of you, my favorite authoress? I would indeed be very grateful and happy to receive one.

With loving regards,
I am
Jewell
Waterloo, Iowa

To My Valentine Laura Ingalls Wilder

Although I've never seen your face,
I feel as though I had,
I've met you in your books, you know,
And they have made me glad.

Anne Mackie

Valentine from Anne Mackie, Chapel Hill, N.C., February 10, 1942 (see page 19)

Class photograph sent by Lee and Clyde, June 3, 1937 (see pages 3–4)
The children are holding up posters they made in school that illustrate scenes from the Little House books.

Pictures made by a Sight Saving class, Cabrillo Avenue School, San Pedro, Calif., January 21, 1942:
"The Indians leaving war camp" in *Little House on the Prairie*
"Feeding the strangers" in *By the Shores of Silver Lake*

Dear Mrs. Wilder,

Here are some notes the class wrote you on your eighty-fifth birthday. Your books continue to be our inspiration to my classes. I add to their congratulations my own and my best wishes.

Birthday cards from the Cabrillo Avenue School, San Pedro, Calif., January 21, 1952

The Little House on the Prairie, made by a fourth grade class out of orange crates and paper, Webster, Wisc., 1944

Family group dressed up as Laura, Pa, Ma, and Mary, Saginaw, Mich., 1944

"At last she sat soberly down to her crocheting." *(from* These Happy Golden Years*) by Gloria, Greenwich, Conn., August 23, 1944 (see page 69)*

"Laura Ingalls Wilder" *by Anne Harrison, Chicago, Ill., April 5, 1945 (see page 70)*

Birthday party for Laura's 80th birthday, Carson Pirie Scott department store, Chicago, Ill., February 7, 1947
Laura was invited by Carson Pirie Scott department store to a celebration in honor of her birthday.
She was unable to attend, but she sent 200 autographs and a letter to the children telling them what had
happened to some of the people she mentioned in her Little House books.

March 29, 1942

Dear Mrs. Wilder,

It's hard to call you Mrs. Wilder. We like to call you Laura. We have read the first four books that you wrote. Are you still writing stories? We like the way you tell your stories. Some places it sounds like poetry. Wasn't it funny when Ma hit the bear and thought it was the cow? We were so happy when you went to church on Chirstmas and got the fur cape. We are sure it was fun to slide on the lake. We would like to know if Mary is still blind. How is Carrie and baby Grace? Have you still got the fiddle that Pa played all the time. We like that fiddle it's a wonderful fiddle.

Coreen
Webber School
Saginaw, Mich.

April 16, 1942

My dear Mrs. Wilder,

   This is a letter of appreciation from the mother of a
nine year old girl who reads everything and your stories
have helped so much to fix ideals and develop a "taste"
in addition to giving reading pleasure.

   In our basement we've had "pioneer homes" and
"covered wagons" (drawn by two very old rocking horses)
and after a rainy day of indoor pioneer play of last week
came these poems by my daughter, which I've enclosed.
I'm keeping the funny down hill written originals for an
aunt who remarks that none of us ever wrote so much as
a jingle!

                                      Respectfully,
                                      Virginia
                                      Cleveland, Ohio

To Make a Pioneer.

To own a buggy
To have a mill.
To master a lot of workman's skill.
Does that? Does that
Make a Pioneer?

To have a Father
That owns an estate.
To make fancy writing on a slate.
Does it? Does it
Make a Pioneer?

To have big horses
And a covered wagon.
To have a dog, his tail a-waggin'
Does that I'm asking you
Make a Pioneer?

No I'll tell you
If ya cant answer me.
A brave heart, courage to strengthen ye
A strong, sweet wife; the will to work.
That's what makes a Pioneer.

Mary Jo Cunningham - 9 yrs old
Written April 1942

Laura

Hair the color of a raven black
Lips as red as roses,
There's no music half so sweet
As her dainty little feet.

Skin as fair as a lily,
Sensible — not silly!
Who could be this person rare
But my little Laura fair?

Mary Jo Cunningham- 9 yrs.

The Prairie.

There's a place far away
That I know till this day.
It's the rambling rolling prairie

Now I sleep in a hot stuffy room.
But I recall a prairie moon.
Now I'm lulled to sleep in a noisy way
But I remember a day
That the cow's moo
And the coyote's yell
Were the only things I had to tell
When I woke up on the prairie.

This I remember and put away
The things I wore;
What I used to play.
In my youthful days on the prairie

Mary Josephine Cunningham
- 9 years old.

37

April 16, 1942

Dear Mrs. Wilder,

I would like to write and tell you how well I enjoyed your books. My teacher read it to all the pupils in our school and we all were so sad to hear that was the last one. So we just couldn't help writing to see if you were writing another book. We all are hoping very much that you will write about when you were a teacher.

I go to a country school, which is about a mile and a half from my home. My teacher's name is Miss Hasse. I live in Sumter which is a very little town.

How many children do you have? Have you any boys or are they all girls? What is Mary doing now, and where does she live? I suppose Grace and Carrie are both grown up now.

I have both brothers and sisters. Two of my brother's are in the army now. I will sign off now as I have school work to do but took off time to write anyway.

Your friend,
Doris
Sumter, Minn.

April 29, 1942

Dear Mrs. Wilder,

Please excuse my writing on lined-paper, but I fear my writing would be very unneat and go up and down if I didn't.

This is the first time I have ever written to an Author (though my brother did) and I only hope my letter is not too boring. I find your books not only exciting, but enjoyable, and they also help me to know of the time when you lived out there (in the West). I know that others that have read your books must enjoy them very much. They are so interesting!

How I wish I could have gone to school with you; you must have been a nice schoolmate. I wish you would write more books about school-teaching, and how you got on.

I am 10, in the sixth grade and I go to an Academy. I'd like to be a school-teacher but I fear I'd never be smart enough. In fact, in your latest book, Little Town on The Prairie, I'd never remember all that History you had to in one of your chapters. I'd probably just get up and sit down again, or pretend I was sick, oh no, I'd never remember all that! My mother (sometimes) complains of having a lot of History to do, but what would she do if I went to school when you did! My favorite subjects are History, Reading, and Spelling. At home I have 3 spelling pins.

I have often thought of writing books of my life or just

fiction, but never did. Everything comes into my mind; in fact, my head swims with it; I'm just getting out the piece of paper and the pen or pencil, when—I forget all! I just can't do it.

I love farm life and horses. It's always been my wish to own several, but, alas, that's only wishing.

Getting back to your books. My father used to read them to me and we'd love the illustrations. Again, I say they're interesting and lovely. Please try to write more, even if it's only one.

I haven't anything else to write so I'll end my letter if you don't mind.

Your Faithful Reader,
Diana
Huguenot Park
Staten Island, N.Y.

P.S. Could you please try to send me a picture of you? I hope so. This is a drawing of a horse:

May 3, 1942

Dear Mrs. Wilder,

I finished your new book about a week ago. And I liked it very much even more then "Long Winter" which I liked too.

You probably don't remember me, but I wrote to you about five months ago and you wrote a nice letter back.

You told me that you were writing a new book, and when it came out I was the first person to get it out of the library.

So I just thought I would write and tell you how much I enjoyed it.

Sincerely Yours,
Marian
Oakland, Calif.

May 24, 1942

Dear Miss Wilder,

I have been reading <u>on</u> <u>the</u> <u>Banks</u> <u>of</u> <u>Plum</u> <u>Creek</u> and
<u>Farmer</u> <u>Boy</u>. Please if you have time write and tell me
about you and your books. If you have a photographs of
yourself please send one too. In our school we have a
free unit. We could work on any one thing we wanted to.
I took you. At home I am a tomboy but at school I try to
be nice or ladylike. I don't seem to make friends in
school. I'm eleven years old and would like to be your
friend.

Your friend,
Bonnie
Detroit, Mich.

August 14, 1942

Dear Laura Ingalls Wilder,

I have enjoyed your books about your girlhood.

My Grandma was born and brought up in Wisconsin too. And my name is Mary and my sisters name is Caroline. I have decided when I grow up and married and have children I am going to name them Laura Mary Carrie and Grace.

Love from
Mary
Santa Barbara, Calif.

P.S. I am 6½ years old

November 3, 1942

Dear Mrs. Wilder,

I am a little girl, thirteen years of age. I have read many, many books, but I still class the pioneer set that you wrote, among my favorites.

I am the proud owner of all the "Laura and Marys," as my sisters and I call them, but we all agree that there should be at least one more book to "marry her off." You see, I usually get one of the set each Christmas, and I don't know what I should do if this Christmas came by without one.

I also would like (if possible) the recipe to sour dough, and sour dough biscuits. They sound so very good that I am dying to taste one.

One of my sisters is 12, the other is 16, and my brother is 18 years old.

I don't know why I am so bold as to write to you, but I am.

So here's lots of love,
and many best wishes
from your true admirer,
Mary
Brooklyn, N.Y.

Laura replied to Mary's letter within a week of receiving it.

Rocky Ridge Farm
Mansfield Missouri
Nov. 12, 1942

My Dear Mary

I am glad that you and your sisters like my books. I have written the "one more book" you want to finish the story. It will be published this month and its title is "These Happy Golden Years."

I hope you get a copy for Christmas and that you like it as well as the others.

Sourdough was really a substitute for sour milk and was used in cooking just as sour milk was.

We had no baking powder in those days and used soda with sour milk or sour dough.

To start it, Mother mixed warm water and flour, a pinch of salt and a little sugar making it about as thick as gravey. This was kept in a warm place until it soured. It was then used as sour milk to make the biscuit but a little of it was left to help start the next batch souring. Enough more water and flour, sugar and salt were added to make enough for use again.

We used it only when we had no milk, which of course is better.

With love
Sincerely yours
Laura Ingalls Wilder

April 5, 1943

Dear Laura,

I hope you don't mind my calling you Laura, but I like to think of you as a little girl.

I have four of your books and enjoy them very much. I like the part best in "By the Shores of Silver Lake" where you see out loud for Mary.

I wonder where Mary is now. I also wonder where you live. How are Grace and Carrie? Will you please write me a letter and tell me how it was to ride in a covered wagon?

From what I've read Pa was a very nice daddy.

I am nine ½ years old and in the fourth grade. I think we study pioneers in the fifth grade.

Lots of Love,
Barbara
Melrose, Mass.

April 17, 1943

My dear Mrs. Wilder,

    I am in the Third Grade at school. We study Pioneer Life. Our teacher has read a number of your books to us. I like "Little House in the Big Woods" best. Our teacher also read that your gingerbread is famous.

    Would you send me your recipe? If you will I shall allow all the rest of the children to copy it. After our mothers have made gingerbread we shall put the recipe in our scrapbooks.

    I was the one chosen by my teacher to make a picture of you in a pink dress with the buggy coming down the street. Thank you for the recipe if you care to send it.

Your true friend,
Madeline
Marion, Ind.

May 22, 1943

Dear Laura,

I like your Books very much. I am very glad you won the prize. I am 6 and ½ I am in the First grade. I cut out your picture from the paper.

Love,
Elizabeth Mary
Brooklyn, N.Y.

I am 6 and ½
I am in the First
grade. I cut out your
picture from the
paper
Love
Elizabeth Mary Plotz

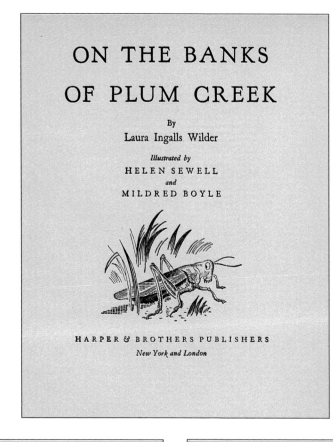

ON THE BANKS
OF PLUM CREEK

By
Laura Ingalls Wilder

Illustrated by
HELEN SEWELL
and
MILDRED BOYLE

HARPER & BROTHERS PUBLISHERS
New York and London

Laura and Mary hurried fast, bringing in wood. Carrie opened the door when they came to it, and shut it behind them. Mary could carry larger armfuls, but Laura was quicker.

They filled the woodbox before it began to snow. The snow came suddenly with a whirling blast, and it was small hard grains like sand.

Bringing all the wood they could stagger under

It stung Laura's face where it struck. When Carrie opened the door, it swirled into the house in a white cloud.

Laura and Mary forgot that Ma had told them to stay in the house when it stormed. They forgot everything but bringing in wood. They ran frantically back and forth, bringing each time all the wood they could stagger under.

"You girls are chilled through. I'll have you a hot drink in a minute," said Ma, hurrying into the kitchen.

She brought them each a steaming cup of ginger tea.

"I CAN'T GET WARM, PA"

"My, that smells good!" said Mary and Grace leaned on Laura's knee looking longingly at the cup till Laura gave her a sip and Pa said, "I don't know why there's not enough of that to go around."

"Maybe there is," said Ma, going into the kitchen again.

The original editions of the Little House books, illustrated by Helen Sewell
On the Banks of Plum Creek *was first published in 1937;* The Long Winter *was first published in 1940.*

Valentine from Seranwyck School, New Castle, Del., June 16, 1947

Laura, Almanzo, and visiting schoolchildren, July 4, 1948
Fans would often stop by Rocky Ridge Farm to catch a glimpse of their beloved author, and Laura always made them feel welcome. One group of fans once arrived on her doorstep around 7 A.M., causing Laura to remark that summer tourists beat even farmers for getting up early! Laura and Almanzo are in the center.

(photo courtesy of William Anderson)

Birthday cards from Grade Six, Kaiulani School, Honolulu, Hawaii, February 2, 1949

"The Little House
in the
Big Woods."

Valentine from the Third Grade, Plainfield School, Plainfield, Ill.,
Drawing by Vivian, 9 years old, February 14, 1949 (see page 104)

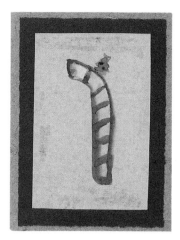

Christmas cards from Atlanta, Ga., December 1952

Laura with visiting schoolgirls, 1952

(photo courtesy of William Anderson)

A classroom dresses up as Little House characters

Laura Ingalls Wilder at age 70
Her publisher sent copies of this autographed picture to her readers
(see page 149).

May 27, 1943

Dear Mrs. Wilder,

I just finished reading "These Happy Golden Years." I had to write and tell you how much I enjoyed it and how verysorry I am that it was the last of the "Little House" books. I have read all of them and liked them because their never seemed to be a dull moment and also because I think the life of our early pioneers is interesting and makes us appreciate our modern conveniences.

I was specially interested in the last book because my great-grandmother taught the first school in the state of Nebraska. I immagine that it was much like the one you taught.

I live in Clinton, Iowa. I am 12 years old and like to read very much. I have read about that school for the blind at Vinton, Iowa although I have never been there.

I would like very much to know in what state you were living when you taught school.

One of your many
devoted readers,
Martha
Clinton, Iowa

May 31, 1943

Dear Mrs. Wilder,

I don't exactly know what to say except to tell you how much I have enjoyed your books. I started reading them when I was nine years old and I am now fifteen years old. I have just finished reading, "These Happy Golden Days" and I thought it was simply marvelous. You have always been my favorite author.

I have in my own bookcase your two latest books and although I have read your other books I am saving a little out of my allowance each week so that when I get married and have children they will not miss your wonderful books.

One of my ambitions is to meet you personally and some time I hope to.

My grandmother will be eighty-one years old this year and when she visited my family last winter she read "The Long Winter" and enjoyed it very much. She also was born in a log cabin.

Please don't think I am silly writing you this. I know I write terrible letters but I wanted to tell you how much I have enjoyed your books and I wish there were many more.

I am sending this to your publishing house as I do not know your address. I truly hope you receive it and have time to write me a short note.

Yours truly,
Susan
Detroit, Mich.

June 5, 1943

Dearest Mrs. Wilder,

Thank you ever so much for the letter. We received it while in North Dakota at the farm it added a lot to the trip.

It is lots of fun to imagine myself doing some of the things you did though I have to admit I would not have known what to do most of the time.

I have enjoyed your books so much that words can't explain it. I think you have given the best description of anything and every thing I have ever read and I read alot for my hobby is reading and collecting stamps. Because of my reading hobby I wish you wouldn't have to stop writing but we all must stop doing certain things after so long.

I also think you have helped a lot of boys and girls become interested in their own state. This winter I took several copies of your books to my teacher and she read them to the class. One of the kids said "I never knew South Dakota had a history like that," after my teacher finished reading the Long Winter. Another said "It makes me cold to read about the winter."

We won't be able to go to DeSmet this spring or summer as we had planned for we had to use our gas along with some supplementary to take the bull to Lilac Hedge the farm in North Dakota, so we are planning for a visit this fall.

School was out Wednesday the 26th of May and for the first time in my life I was awfully glad it was out. Next year I will go to Junior High.

In all the fairs, horse show etc. I have seen I've never seen a pair of horses that could equal your description of Mr. Wilder's Morgans. They must have been about the most beautiful horses on earth. I would have liked to have ridden or driven Prince and Lady for I love horses and I think I know good ones when I see them or hear of them but maybe not.

Sincerely yours,
Sylvia Adelaide
Watertown, S.D.

P.S. Is a covered wagon easier for a tall girl to ride in than a car?

June 12, 1943

Dear Mrs. Wilder,

I want to tell you how much I have enjoyed your books. I call them the "Laura and Mary books," and they are my favorites. I think you must be the "Laura" in the story. I love you very much. I still have the last two books to read. I am eight years old.

Sincerely yours,
Irene Adrienne
Altadena, Calif.

September 3, 1943

Dear Mrs. Wilder,

I don't exactly know how to begin this letter as I feel I know you instead of being a total stranger to you. You see, I have read each of your books many times and you seem more like one of my friends.

I am a girl, 14 years of age, and your books have brought a great deal of enjoyment to me, so I am writing this letter to try and explain what they've meant to me.

In your books, you have told how you, as a girl, felt about the open prairie and being free to run on it like the wind. Even though I can't put it in words I feel the same way.

I just finished your latest book, and I really cried when I saw it was the last one, but I suppose all good things must come to an end.

I hope so very much that you read this letter and understand how I feel, because I guess only an author can put on paper what he feels in his heart. As I am not or even hope to be the author you are, I hope you can sort of read between the lines and understand how I feel about you and the wonderful books you wrote. Since I read your first book I thought you must be a strong and courageous woman and I'm sure you are. I would be so very happy and honored if you would answer this letter.

A very ardent admirer,
Pat
Portland, Ore.

October 3, 1943

Dear Mrs. Wilder,

I am a young girl 10 years old. I am writing to tell you how very much I enjoyed your books of your life in pioneer days.

The first book I heard about was read to me by my Mother when I was ill in bed last winter. It was so good I decided to get the rest of the books you wrote. Now I am hoping to have the set for my very own.

While I was ill in bed I got a beautiful doll which I named Laura after you.

I think I shall always remember your books and the people in them—even Nellie Oleson.

Do you think you would ever have time to write to me? I would so much like to hear from you.

Sincerely yours,
Anita Marie
Bellingham, Wash.

December 21, 1943

Dear Mrs. Wilder,

For a number of years, I have used your series of children's books in my classroom. I think you will be interested in reading the reactions of my present pupils.

Sincerely,
Mildred K. Bickel
Teacher, Shore School
Euclid, Ohio

Dear Mrs. Wilder,

Our class has made a hobby of reading your books. There is one thing I want to know. Is Laura supposed to be you, or are your books a story of your life?

By Barbara

I like your stories very much. They are so like true life. Most stories I do not like because the boys and girls are so good. I also like the way you describe the things they do. You may think that because I am ten years old I cannot enjoy books like that, but I really enjoy your books.

By Ira

P.S. Please write more.

I like the L. H. in the B. W. because Laura is sucha tomboy and Mary is such a lady. I like the stories pa tells in the evening by the fireplace. It makes me feel like I was right there with them.

By Jaquelyn

I liked Laura in the story best because she would play with all the boys that came to visit them. I liked it because it sounded as though it were real and Mary and Laura were right beside you.

By Bob

I like your books because some things happened to them. They get hurt and have many hardships.

By Bob

I like your stories because you make them such real life and it is not our usual life. Whenever we have a book report I always say, "May I have a Wilder book?" Mrs. Wilder, please write more books.

By Mary Ellen

I enjoy Laura and Mary books. I like them because Laura always gets into things. Please write more.

By Nancy

January 10, 1944

Dear Mrs. Wilder,

Your books have interested me very much. I have
read them all and they are wonderful.

Are Mary, Carrie, and Grace fiction characters or real
people? If so, are they still living?

My Grandfather has been through the same "Long
Winter" that you talk about. He was in Pipestone County
then. He says he had to endure the same hardships as
you. He had to grind wheat, twist hay, and many other
things. I thank you for writing such interesting books for
boys and girls.

A friend,
Raymond
Minneapolis, Minn.
Age, 10 yrs.

Jan. 27, 1944

Dear Mrs. Wilder

I have read all your your books except On The
Banks Of Plum Creek which doesn't seem to be
in the 42nd Street Library. I was very ~~happy~~ excited
when I read the book Hard Winter. I wondered
how you lived through all those blizzards. How
come the winds didn't blow your house away? How
did you feel when you had to be a school
teacher because ~~no~~ Mary was blind? I feel very
sorry for her. My little twin sisters want to
know if Grace, Carrie and Mary are still living.
Do you still want to get even with you teacher
Eliza Jane Wilder because she did those mean
things to Carrie? I wish you could write some
books about the life of Carrie and Grace later
on. I think Grace was cute when she asked
Pa if his nose is ~~foz~~ frozen. Weren't you
afraid when you ~~slide~~ slid on Silver Lake and
saw the big Buffalo Wolf? If I was in your
place then I would be so scared that I'd
run away without Carrie. You were real
brave to wait for Carrie. I wish I lived
with you all through your life.

Yours Truly

Emily Mazur

May 4, 1944

Dear Mrs. Wilder,

 I am 8 years old and in the second grade. Mother read me the Little House Books you wrote and we just loved them.

 I have a hair doll and sometimes I fixed her up to look like Ma and Mary and you.

I love you,
Beverly
Seattle, Wash.

Dear Mrs. Wilder,
I am 8 years old
and in the second
grade. Mother
read me the Little
House Books you
wrote and we just
loved them.

May 24, 1944

Dear Laura,

    I know you are not a little girl any more but it seems like you still are. I bought the book On The Banks Of Plum Creek. I think that your books are the best books I have read because I learned a lot. my best girl friend Carol dosen't like true books so you do not have to worry that I dont.

    Sincerely yours,
Jean
Milwaukee, Wisc.

August 23, 1944

Dear Mrs. Wilder,

I recived your letter two weeks ago, it was a nice letter and the first letter I ever got besides postcards and birthday cards and my first business letter from the Audubon Society. I determined I got such few letters that I would save them all, speicelly yours.

I made a picture of you in a spigged dress and your hair in braids notted in the back.

It's too bad that Charlotte burned up. It was sad to hear that because I know you tresured it alot.

I supose you like living on a farm where there are alot of wild animals & birds. My sister (Christine) and I love to study nature, we like birds, flowers, and we like to study the stars at night.

Well my hands are getting tired and besides it's dinner time so I close this letter.

Sincerely yours,
Gloria
Greenwich, Conn.

P.S. I am sending the picture to you.

(See page 30 for Gloria's picture of Laura.)

November 6, 1944

Dear Mrs. Wilder,

    Although I am only nine years old I have read every one of your little house books and enjoyed them very, very much. So have papa and Mama. We feel that we know you and your family very much and love you all, Laura the most. We are very eager to know more about your people in later years, so won't you please write another book and tell what happened to Ma and Pa and Carrie and Grace and Almanzo? Especially Mary, we are so anxious to know about her.

    With deep thanks for the many happy hours spent with you and your family,

                    Most Sincerely,
                    Mary
                    Ithaca, N.Y.

April 3, 1945

Dear Mrs. Wilder,

    My name is Anne. I am eight years old.

I live in Chicago. I have read all the books you wrote.

I like Little house on the Prairie and Farmer boy best.

                    your friend,
                    Anne
                    Chicago, Ill.

April 13, 1945

Dear Mrs. Wilder,

No doubt you will be much surprised to hear from a little boy living way up here in Northern Minnesota. We have lots of big woods here to and I think the pines are so pretty. Last fall, my teacher started reading books to us in school. Among them was one of your book's The little House In The Big Wood's. Since them there have been several other's. I believe she is now reading the fourth one of your book's. It is "On the Banks of Plum Cireek." I like the stories so much. I some times borrow the book's from my teacher. Then in the evenings my mother read's to my little sister an me. Joyce likes your stories too and she talks all the time about Baby Carrie. She must have been a sweet baby. Do you still live in the country and have you any big wood's near by? I use to live in the Red River Valley and liked that country so much Daddy says we will go back some day. I hope you are well and if you can spare a little time I wish you would write to me some time. Mother say's she feels almost as if we really know you now. Thank's for all the good book's. Please write more of them soon.

Your friend,
Norman
Bemidji, Minn.

P.S. I am in the fourth grade.

June 20, 1946

Dear Mrs. Wilder,

I feel like I have known you all my life because I have read all your books.

I got your address from Barbara a girl who I take music lessons with.

I have a brother 8, a sister 2½, and I will be 11 in August.

My girl friends and I act out your stories and make them in to plays. Sometimes we play them in our log cabin that daddy built for us from logs he got when he cut down some trees.

We live 6 miles from any stores. We are right on the Mississippi River.

Your friend,
Betsy
Minneapolis, Minn.

September 25, 1946

Dear Mrs. Wilder,

Our children's Librarian at Winfield, Kansas, told us you lived in Mansfield, Mo. For a long time I thought I would write to you and tell you how much how much I love to read the little house books.

We have been on a long trip. We went to De Smet. Mr. Sherwood at the news paper office told us where to find your homestead. Daddy took some pictures. We will send you some when we get the prints. We wanted to go to Pepin when we were at Rochester but our grandfather was there and did not feel like taking that long a ride.

The first of our trip we went through Independence where Mr. Edwards met Santa Claus.

We are at Green Mountain Falls, Colorado. In a week we will go to my Grandmothers in Dodge City, Kansas. My Daddy has been Dean of Southwestern College in Winfield. At conference next month he will be sent to be the preacher in another town.

I have a big brother Robert who is eleven and a little sister Barbara who is four. I am nine. I will send you a picture of us all.

your friend,
Margaret
Winfield, Kans.

January 6, 1947

Dear Mrs. Wilder,

    Our teacher has been reading to us the eight books
that you wrote, beginning with "Little House in the Big
Woods". All of us like these books very much. We like
them because it makes us forget that we are sixth graders
in Longfellow School and makes us feel as if we were
pioneers on the prairie. Some of us who didn't like
History before now like it a great deal. We all like Ma
because she was so refined and dependable. We think Pa
was a real good scout. Some of us cried when Jack died
and Mary was blind. Every day we wait for story time to
see what happened next.

    We would like a picture of you. Will you send us one?
There are thirty children in our class and every one feels
as if we know you.

                                    Sincerely,
                                    Sixth Grade
                                    Longfellow School
                                    La Crosse, Wisc.

March 20, 1947

Dear Mrs. Wilder,

    I have heard your stories and I have enjoyed them. I like the "Happy Golden Years" best. I have heard three stories of Almanzo. The teacher is reading the "Farmer Boy."

    We have school out here. Some children come to school on carts, some in wheelchairs, and some with crutches, and some walk. We have school just like other boys and girls.

    My name is Dorothy. I have blue eyes and light brown hair. I am nine. I am in the 4B. I am four feet tall. I like to read, write, spell, and do Arithmetic. I like to write and read best. I lit the Christmas tree at the City Hall on Christmas Eve. I got a Bride doll which I love.

                                   Your friend,
                                   Dorothy
                                   Children's Hospital
                                   Convalescent Home
                                   Farmington, Mich.

March 21, 1947

Dear Mrs. Wilder,

We were very happy to get your nice letter. It made us feel like we really know you.

It is too bad that you and Almanzo were sick but we are glad that you are well again. Many of us had to miss school because of the flu.

It made us sad to hear that Mary and Carrie have died.

The publishers sent us a nice picture of you. We think you are pretty. Miss Socolofsky bought a frame for your picture. We set it on a table with some of your books. Above the table is a bulletin board with your letter and the letter from the publishers.

We had fun drawing pictures about things that happened in your books.

Our teacher is going to read <u>Farmer Boy</u> soon.

With love to your from your friends,
The Third Grade
Theodore Roosevelt School
Manhattan, Kans.

The following four letters came from a single family in Harrold, S.D., and arrived in one envelope at Rocky Ridge.

April 8, 1947

Dear Laura,

I have read all of your books.

The one I liked best was "These Happy Golden Years." I liked By The Banks of Plum Creek, too. I am 9½ years old. I am Bettie Ann of Harrold, S. Dak.

I am in the fourth grade.

It is about 2:00 o'clock

We sure enjoy your books.

This is not a very long letter but it will do. Well, good by.

Love,
Bettie Ann

May 1, 1947

Dear Laura,

I like to hear your books read to me. I am in the 2nd grade.

Robert

May 1, 1947

Dear Laura,
    Thank you.
    Good books.
    I like them.
    I am seven years old.

Merrill

May 7, 1947

Dear Laura,
    I call you Laura because it seem as tho I've known you for years. I've read every one of your books and I love them all. I hated most of all to read "These Happy Golden Years." Do you know why? Because it was the last book you wrote and if I could have my way I would have asked you to keep on writing books of yourself. I wish you could keep on. I am sure that every one that read your books loves them My sisters and I do. What is Carrie's, Mary's and Grace's address and what is their names now? Oh, please tell me.
    I wish you would please write to me. Would you please send me a card with your name written on it to me. And if you do write it please write it yourself.

Love and luck,
Mary Kathleen

Newark Del.
June 5, 1947

Dear Laura,
I liked your books.
They were wonderful.
I especially liked it when Nellie
Oleson got the bloodsuckers on her.
It was funny when you and Mary
got on the hay stack when you were not
suppose to get on it.
It was sad when Mary went blind.
It was also sad when Jack died.
We would love you to come and visit us
if you can.
A boy named Skip cried when he
heard Jack died.
We all like you we think you are one
of the nicest ladies we every knew.
I am in second grade and I am going on
to third.
                    Love Kay Nahn

79

November 12, 1947

Dear Mrs. Wilder,

I do wish that I were you, because I'd like to run and play on the vast prairie instead of living in a crowded city.

I think I'd like living in a dugout as you did when you were young.

To watch the rippling creek go slowly on its way must have been beautiful in comparison with the noisy crowded city life.

Wasn't it great fun to slide down the hay-stack and to watch the big clumsy cattle being driven to their pastures on the prairies.

I am looking forward to reading other books that you have written.

Sincerely yours,
Guy
Prescott School
Syracuse, N.Y.

540 Bryant Avenue
Syracuse 4, New York
November 20, 1947

Dear Mrs Wilder,

Your book "The Long Winter" is one of the most interesting books I have ever read. I like an exciting book, and since those things have really happened it doubles the pleasure. When you and Carrie were coming home from school in the storm, the way you decribed it, it sent chills up and down my backbone.

Weren't you pretty young to get a teachers certificate? Nowadays we have to go through college. My teacher even took a course in learning how to mark papers.

Someday I hope to have read all your books.

Your friend,
Patricia Sage

January 18, 1948

Dear Mrs. Wilder,

   We have read all your books.

   We have two of our own.

   The one's we have are Little House in the Woods and Farmer Boy

   We especially Like These Happy Golden years. We went to California the summer of 1947. We stopped in De Smet, Keystone and Pierre and went to the Newspaper office and got Mr. Sherwood in De Smet. He showed us all around even out on the prairie Where you lived in the summer. We were surprized to see that your Pa's store was now turned into a house

   It is too bad that Silver lake is dried up We went around much more than this But I can not tell all of it on this letter. Next we went to Pierre. We saw Pa's fiddle there

   Then to Keystone. We saw Carries house. She passed away before we got there though. We would like to hear from you telling us more about your life. Please.

   I am nine and my sister is six. When we read the books we were 5 and 8. They are the most interesting books we've ever read

   Our Mother and Father and Grandparents enjoyed them too

   My name is Jimmie. My sisters name is Peggy

                                        Yours Sincerely,
                                        James and Peggy
                                        Minneapolis, Minn.

February 4, 1948

Dear Mrs. Wilder,

My teacher has ben reading books of you and your family. I like them very much. We have just eaten supper. I have three sisters and no brothers. My oldest sister is in sixth grade and she is 11 years old. Her name is Marilyn. My next oldest sister is in first grade and she is 7 years old. Her name is Shirley. My youngest sister is only 10 months old and next Saturday she will be 11 months old. Her name is Linda. I am 9 years old. My name is Kenneth. I am left handed. My baby sister is going to be left-handed too. I just got through drying dishes for my mother. My baby sister is playing with a tin cup and it makes me think of the Christmas when you got a tin cup and a penny. Please write to me. I hope you are well. My sister has the mumps and now I may get them to.

I'M going to be an artist when I get big

I didn't trace it

Kenneth

Kenneth
Knox, Ind.

March 31, 1948

Dear Laura,

I am writing to thank you for giving me such enjoyment. I always wanted to live in the olden days and be a teacher and you explained it so well that I feel like it happened to me. I feel very sorry about your family and about Mary's blindness, because you see, I have a sister who is 15 yrs. and she has been wearing glasses since she was 18 mo. I am 13, I have a brother 17 and a pair of twins 7 There are 5 in all. You are very lucky because you lived when they didn't have such things as cars, washing machines, moving pictures and such. Laura, tell me truthfully did you like the olden days better than you do now? If I were you I would. On Christmas in the olden days it must have been fun to hide the things you were making and then give them out. From now on whenever I get in trouble or in doubt about anything I am just going to stop and think what you did when you got in a scramble. I would be very happy if you would write to me and tell me about yourself Almanzo and Rose! I hope this letter finds you in good health.

I am,
your friend,
Judy
Brooklyn, N.Y.

April 19, 1948

Dear Mrs. Wilder,

We have been studying about social letters in language. We were going to write a letter to someone so our teacher suggested we write to you. Our whole class happily agreed with her for we have all enjoyed your books so very much. Our teacher reads your books to us. When she finishes reading a book I read it to my brother. He enjoys them so very much.

We do not have "Little House in the Big Woods" in our library at school so I have not read it yet. I wish you would write more books for I could never get tired of reading them.

There isn't anyone of your books I like better than the others. They are all so good I just couldn't pick between any of them.

Admiringly yours,
Beatrice
Roosevelt School
Maywood, Ill.

April 21, 1948

Dear Mrs. Wilder,

I enjoy your books very much. The first time I read them I didn't read them in order. When I saw that they were in a series, well, that was a good excuse to read them over again. Now our teacher is reading us the whole series. But I really enjoy them more each time. She hasn't read "Those Happy Golden Years" yet but she will soon. As for me, I wish there were other books following it.

I like your books because they are true. They just have something in them that makes you want to read the next one. Another reason I like them is because I can visualize the characters. Ma with Grace in her lap sitting in the rocking chair. Pa playing his fiddle. And calm, sweet, Mary sewing fine, tiny, even stitches in a handkerchief.

Your faithful admirer,
Pat
Roosevelt School
Maywood, Ill.

Kaiulani School

783 North King St.

Dear Mrs. Wilder   May 5, 1948

    I have read many of your books, which
I borrowed from the library of our school.
Now I'm reading one of your books call "The
Long Winter". I have already finished reading
"Little House in The Big Woods" "Little House
on the Prairie" "On The Banks of Plum Creek"
and "By The Shores of Silver Lake." All of the
books were very interesting I have enjoyed them
very much. Many other children are also enjoying
reading your books.

    I am a Chinese boy I came from
China about two years ago. Now I am in
the fifth grade and working hard. I have
just started to enjoy reading books. I like
your books the best because they are so
interesting and exciting. I hope someday
you will come to Hawaii and write a
story about us.

             Mahalo

             Johnson Yee

Dacotah St. School
May 7, 1948

Dear Laura,

I like your books very much.
I like the reason for your being a
school teacher — so you could help
Mary to go to college. I really think
you have a marvelous mind to
remember all these things.

I think that Ma was a
good Mother. She never complained
about anything.

I think Pa was jolly
and he never complained either. I
don't think anybody complained in your
family. But they had plenty to complain
about.

I think you were brave in
the blizzard when you had to
come home from school. I'm sure
glad you got home safely. I think
you were also brave the time
when you saw the wolf. I'm glad
the wolf didn't run after you.

                    Sincerely,
                Sandra Simonick

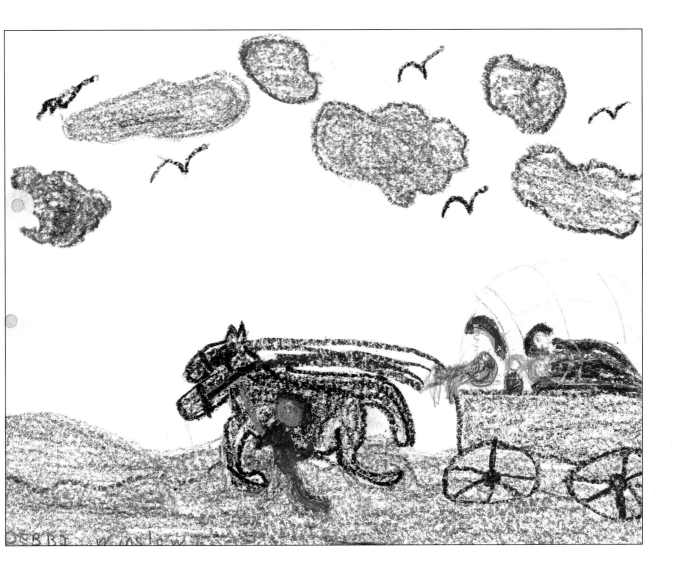

Drawings from Grade Four, Seymour Jackson School, Seymour, Ind., 1951
"Crossing the River on the Way to the Prairie" *by Debbi Winslow*

"Little House on the Prarie" *by Lindy H.*

"Little House on the Prairie" *by Daniel*

"The Prairie Fire in the book Little House on the Prairie" *by Kevin Aker*

Wheels of Fire from On the Banks of Plum Creek
Brad Prather

"Wheels of Fire from On the Banks of Plum Creek" *by Brad Prather*

The part I like best is in one of Laura's books, On the Bank of Plum Creack. The part I like best is when the cattle come and eat pa's haystacks.

"The cattle in Pa's haystacks" *by Veronica*

"Laura and Mary, Little Plum Creek" *by Kathy*

Laura signing books in Springfield, Missouri, 1952
Laura's last public appearance was at Brown's Bookstore in Springfield.
Nearly eighty-six years old, she generously autographed her books for lines of admiring fans.

May 8, 1948

Dear, dear mrs. Wilder,

    My brother and I are so happy we can write you how much we enjoy your books and love you for writing them. They are so exciting and real. They are the most interesting books we have ever read. I wish we could have spent a summer with you in your claim Shanty. poor dear Mary's eyes made me cry. I like to "play like" she could see some day. Have you still the little china Shepherdess? I think we liked most of all "The little house on the prairie." John and I hope in these years you are well and happy. You have made so many children happy with your wonderful stories. God love you.

Your devoted children,
Rosiland (age 8)
John (age 7)
Wichita, Kans.

May 12, 1948

Dear Laura,

    I am putting you name Laura because we read so
much about you that you seem like you are a young
friend to me.

    Mrs. Maddock our teacher is reading us about The
Little Town On The Prairie.

    I guess you haven't forgot how to twist haw and
remember how you had to eat brown bread and potatoes.

    In one book Mrs. Maddock read us, you and Almasoal
got married and everyone laughted when Almasoal and
you were kissing in the moon light.

    Well, I guess I will close now.

                        Love your friend,
                        truly,
                        Joanne
                        Beulah, Mich.

May 13, 1948

Dear Laura,

 I like your books because they're so exciting, and so interesting. Our teacher reads us a chapter everyday and we can't wait til tomorrow to find out what happens. I am writing this letter because I think your books are just wonderful. Our teachers used to let us take books home and I took the book home called Little House on the Prairie. I didn't want to stay in and read because I wanted to stay outside and play with my friends, but when our teacher started reading the book I couldn't believe that six people could have so much excitement. It was so interesting. If I had lived then I probably wouldn't have had half of the excitement you did. Now that I have told you how much I enjoy your books I would like to ask a few questions. Were you and Mary surprised when the balls of fire started coming in your home? There's one thing I think is surprising. It's the way Mary was about her eye's. She never complained. Is anyone in your family still living besides you? I do hope you can find time to write to me.

Sincerely yours,
Donna Rose
Dacotah Street School
Los Angeles, Calif.

May 29, 1948

Dear Laura,

If I could I would gladly trade lives with you except, maybe, for the hard winter you had. You were brave when you had to eat the same things every day and when you had to stay inside next to the stove and listen to the blizzard winds screaming. Most children wouldn't be satisfide and would make a big fuss over eating and doing the same things every day. Ma and Pa were good sports and they hardly ever complained when things went wrong.

I think one of the most interesting parts in the books so far was when you went on your first train ride. It must have been exciting.

It was too bad that Mary went blind, when she wanted to be a teacher so much. It was awfully nice of you to be sort of a teacher to her and help her to learn things so she would keep up with you and someday go to the College For The Blind. And I'm glad she went.

Our class has been reading your books and they seem to tell more than our history books do. We have read six of your books and we are in the middle of The Little Town on the Praire.

Sincerely yours,
Sandy
Dacotah Street School
Los Angeles, Calif.

October 28, 1948

Dear Mrs. Wilder,

　　I am a girl 10 years and in sixth grade.

　　When I first read your books I though "Those are neat books." The first one I read was These Happy Golden Years. Your books are very interesting.

　　One thing you should write more books about after you were married to Mr. Wilder.

　　I hope you like this writing paper. My grandmother sent it to me. I picked it because it might remind you of walking through fields with Mary.

　　I am enclosing a picture of myself at Camp Ojiketoa Camp Fire Girl camp.

Your friend forever,
Prudence
(Prudy for short)
St. Paul, Minn.

January 31, 1949

Dear Mrs. Wilder,

    Do you still like to slide down the haystack. When the teacher read it we laughed and we couldn't stop laughing. We didn't think it was very nice when Nellie teased you.

                    You Friend,
                    JoAnne
                    Grant School
                    Moline, Ill.

February 3, 1949

Dear Mrs. Wilder,

I am 11 years old, and I have everyone of your books except the last one and I just love them. The first time I knew about them was when I was in third grade, and my teacher read us The Little House in the Big Woods, and told us that Laura was a real little girl, I was so glad when I knew that you were Laura and it was your own folks you wrote about. I got "The Little Town on the Prairie" for Christmas, and now I can hardly wait to read "Those Happy Golden Years," but I feel so bad because it is the last one.

My mother and I were talking about you the other day, and she said why don't we find where you lived so I could write you a letter and tell you how much I love your stories. So we called the library and they gave us your address and said your birthday is on February 7 so I am sending you a bithday card. My Grandma lives with us and she is as old as you are. She likes to read my books because she can remember about some of the things you wrote about. She lived in Ohio when she was a little girl, on a farm too. I am going to keep all your book, because if I ever have a little girl she will just love them like I do. After I read the last book I think I will start over again. I hope you have a very nice birthday.

Do you think maybe you could write me a little note and I keep it in one of my books.

Your Friend,
Marilyn Lee
Des Moines, Iowa

February 11, 1949

Dear Laura,

    Our teacher is reading your story of <u>The</u> <u>Little</u> <u>House</u> <u>in</u> the <u>Big</u> <u>Woods</u> to us. We like it very much. We say "Read more!" when it is time for her to stop reading.

    The way you lived when you were a little girl is very much like the way our great grandparents lived around here. So your story helps us to understand life around Plainfield many years ago.

    We hope you had a happy birthday on February 7th. We are late with our birthday wishes because our school was closed for nine days on account of icy roads. It was not safe for our school buses to travel over the country roads.

    Vivian, one of our classmates, made this valentine for you.

    We hope you are well.

> Admirers of the Laura Books
> Third Grade
> Plainfield School
> Plainfield, Ill.

(See page 53 for Vivian's valentine.)

March 2, 1949

Dear Laura,

    We have read your good books and we think they are very fine. We hope you don't mind us calling you Laura as we feel we know you by that name. We felt we should write you a letter because you had become so real to us. We hope you will answer this letter and send us your picture. We also wish to know about Carrie, Grace, and Mary.

    We like your style of writing because we can picture the story in our minds as if we were there with you.

    Thank you for writing such wonderful books for the children of America.

> Your friends,
> The Third Grade
> Pordeaux School
> Shelton, Wash.

These are your friends.

Sandra	Donald	Dee	Charles
Cathy	Stanley	Jimmy	Roberta
Reed	Harley	Sandra	John
Carol	Betsy	Nancy	Kenneth
Carol	Sharon	Randall	Marshall
Patricia	Everett	Larry	
Romona Mae	Karen	Carl	
Arlene	Johnny	Marlene	

March 21, 1949

Dear Laura,

I am a little girl 10 years old. I'm in the fifth grade at school. I go to a country school not far from home so I can run home for dinner every day. I have taken piano lessons for four years. I also go to the Lutheran Sunday School and Church. In summer I go to Bible School.

I have read all your books and I like them very much. I took them home from school and my Mother, Daddy and Brother read them. We like them so much that we all read them every winter. Daddy says we can live them all over again they are so real.

On our farm we have cows, horses, pigs, sheep, and chickens. We have electricity and live on a good road, but we don't have a bathroom. So in winter days we have to get the tub in the kitchen by the range to take a bath. Then we always say we're back in the Mary and Laura days.

Mother says I shouldn't have written "Dear Laura," but I have read the books so often I feel that I know you as a little girl. I like to walk in the field and pick flowers as you did and help feed cows, chickens, and ride my pony. I'm afraid I'm not quite as good as Mary though. Mother says I can't sit still long enough.

We went to Vinton last summer so we drove passed the school of the blind where Mary went.

If it is not asking too much I wish you would write to me and tell me what Mary did when she came home from school and about Carrie and Grace. Did Pa and Ma stay on the claim or did they move West? Most of all I want to know all about you, Laura. Did you stay in the house Almanzo built for you? And did you have any children, and all about your married life. We are very much interested.

We are going to get a set of your books so we can read our own in the winter and I would like to put your letter in your last book to read.

We could just see you and Almanzo go buggy riding. I bet it was fun. Did Almanzo keep on with his horses and farming. I could just keep on asking more and more questions, but I guess I had better stop or you will get tired reading them.

I want to thank you very much for reading my letter and I hope you find time to answer it. Again I want to say of all the books I have ever read I like yours best because they are so very real. Thank you again,

Doreen Marie
Anamosa, Iowa

April 12, 1949

Dear Mrs. Wilder,

Our teacher, Miss Davis has been reading your books. We think they are all very nice but the one I especially like is the one of Indian territory. Miss Davis is just finishing <u>These</u> <u>Happy</u> <u>Golden</u> <u>Years</u>.

My hobby is collecting pennies, and building airplanes, and I like to read, too.

We read an article in the Kansas City Star, about your being 82, years old.

We wish you a very happy Easter.

Yours Truly,
Kenneth
Louisa May Alcott School
Kansas City, Kans.

6352 S. Sangamon St.
Chicago 21, Ill.
June 3, 1949

Dear Laura,

We're going to call you Laura because we've learned to love you by that name. We're the Third Grade at Our Lady of Solace School in Chicago. We've read all about your life in the Little House Books. We'll have to wait a few years to finish the next three. Would you please tell us what happened to all your sisters, Mary, Carrie and Grace? The only thing we don't like about your books is they are too short and there aren't enough of them. Our school is out June 9. We'd like our last day-of-school-treat to be a letter from you, Please?

Your little friends who also live in little houses.

Third Grade
Gloria Lett

109

Wewoka, Oklahoma
November 23, 1949

Dear Laura,

We are telling the things we are thankful for and we want you to know that all our boys and girls are very thankful for your books and love you for writing them for us.

your friends,

Mary Francis   Bernice
Peggy Lynn   Alvie
Katherine Payne   Jerry
Tish Moore   Larry
Jimmie Little   Ray
Linda Sue Epton   Judy
Patsy Ann   Lynda
Lou Alice Tilley   FLOYD
Gayle   Gerald
Judy   Joyce Muir
Shirley Jean   Jimmie Dale
Patsy O'Loughlin Thomas
                      Ronald

February 4, 1952

Dear Mrs. Wilder,

    I have read all of your books. I enjoyed them so much. They were exciting in some places, thrilling, pleasing and so many other things.

    How I got started reading them was that my grandfather gave me "Little House In The Big Woods" and I liked it so much I read the whole series.

    I am in the Sixth Grade. Reading is one of my favorite things to do.

    Our teacher (Mrs. Booth) made reading charts for everyone. At the end of the month we see who has read the most books. Last month Richard read the most and I read the second most. I wish I had more time to read but I have three little sisters and I don't have much time to read except in the evenings.

    You must have had lots of fun when you were little.

    I hope you have a very nice birthday.

Sincerely,
Julie
Palm School
Riverside, Calif.

February 4, 1952

Dear Mrs. A. J. Wilder,

    I wish you a happy birthday on the seventh of
February. I wish I had the magic to make you young
again. If I did I would give it all to you because 85 is an
awful old age to be and I don't think I'll like it when I
get that old.

    I think the best book you wrote was "Little House in
The Big Woods."

Yours truly,
Bill
Palm School
Riverside, Calif.

Dear Mrs Wilder
    I _____ books. We like them.
We do _____ work in our r___
I appreciate you _____

We are ___
___
___

Boulevard School
___field California

___ House

River Boulevard School
Bakersfield California
April 29, 1952

Dear Mrs Wilder,
    We enjoyed your books about you and
your family. The teacher read all
the books ekept one. We enjoy them very
much. We were glad to get the letter. I missed
school that day when the letter came. I missed
Mrs. Hort to read the stories about you.
We do many things in our room. We do word work
and. We paint and we sew. We do cooking. We make
candy and cake jello and cut cake and lots of
other kinds of food in our Special Training
Class. We are going to have an open house night.
Tuesday April 29, 1952 We are going to display
the best work that we did in our room.
I hope you will get well soon. Is Mary alive?
I hope she is. We will like the book that Mrs.
Hort is reading to us now. It is The Little
House in the Big Woods.
                Your friend
                Albert Gonzales

Letters from River Boulevard School, Bakersfield, Calif., April 29, 1952 (see page 134)

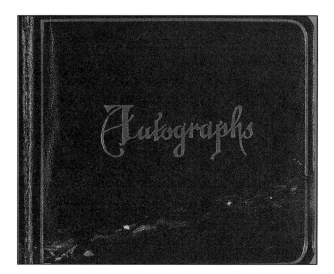

> Dear Mrs. Wilder,
>
> I hope you are well?
> I love the stories in the books.
> I remember when Mary went
> to college. I knew you missed
> her very very much. Thank you,
>
> Linda Cox

> Dear Mrs. Wilder,
> Laura, brown curls
> are just as pretty as
> blond curls. Did you
> have fun playing with
> the pig's tail? I love your
> books very much. I wish
> you would write more
> books. Thank you
> Sandra Rush

Autograph album from Grade Five, Theodore Roosevelt School, Compton, Calif., June 1953 (see pages 135–36)
Autographs by Linda Cox and Sandra Rush

Dear Mrs Wilder
          Our room
is all most finished with
all of the books. We are
reading the book of "The
Little Town on the Prairie".
We have enjoyed all of your
books. Do you remember when
you got the blood suckers

Dear Mrs. Wilder,
          I have been reading your
books and I enjoy them very
much. I have read three of
them. My teacher has read all
of them but one to my class.
I like "The Little Town on
the Prairie" very much.
                    Alfred Boegh

Dear Mrs Wilder,
I enjoy you books very much. Mrs
Keeney, my teacher, is reading
them to my class and all of the
other children enjoy them as much
as I do.
                    Yours truly,
                    Diane Williams

Autographs by Bill Ishmael, Alfred Boegh, and Diane Williams

Happy Birthday

Feb 7
Birthday

Mansfield farm

Car

Hoyt School
Saginaw Mich.
Feb. 7, 1957

Dear Mrs. Wilder

I go to Hoyt School in Saginaw Mich. And my teacher's name is Miss Stineman. And I am in the fifth grade room 203. I am ten myself. And I read a lot of books. But you are my favorite writer. I have read a good many stories of yours and they are very good. I have five of your books and there are some books at school. I think the Little House in the Big Woods is the most exciting of all your stories I wish you a very happy birthday and all the luck in the world

Your friend
Floyd Forongo.

Books

Heart

Missouri

To you

Birthday letter from Floyd Forongo, Hoyt School, Saginaw, Mich., February 7, 1957 (see page 142)

Hoyt School
Saginaw, Mich
Feb 7, 1957

Dear Mrs. Wilder

I wish you a happy Birthday.
I am Delmar W. Goff
I am in the fifth grade
I read four of your books.
They are wonderful books to
read.

With love
Delmar W. Goff.

Birthday letter from Delmar W. Goff, Hoyt School, Saginaw, Mich., February 7, 1957

Hoyt School
Saginaw Mich
Feb 2 1957

Dear Mrs. Wilder
I know that today is your birthday so I want to wish you a very HAPPY BIRTHDAY. My name is Nancy Lynn Dean + as you can see I go to Hoyt School. My age is ten (10). "By the Banks of Plum Creek" is my favorite book of yours.
Getting back to myself. I have two (2) fish named Comet + Star. I also have a turtle named

Birthday letter from Nancy Dean, Hoyt School, Saginaw, Mich., February 7, 1957 (see page 145)

Rocky Ridge Farm
(*photo © 1994 by Leslie A. Kelly*)

Laura's writing desk, on display at Rocky Ridge Farm

(photo © 1994 by Leslie A. Kelly)

February 28, 1952

Dear Laura,

 We have all enjoyed reading your books. We feel that we know you and want to write to you.

 Our school began September 17th and will close for summer vacation June 13th. We have two weeks vacation at Christmas and one week vacation in April. Our school day is from 9:00 p.m. to 3:15 a.m. with an hour for lunch.

 We have been studying western movement in the United States. We are now studying modern California. We go to the auditorium every week to watch educational sound movies.

 We have a puppet stage which is eight feet long and three feet wide.

 Our physical education coach comes once in two weeks to teach us new games.

 We have a piano in our room and we like to sing.

 Every Friday we have a test in Spelling. We enjoy reading and we make book reports. We are learning to use the dictionary. We are studying fractions.

 We usually have warm sunny weather here in California.

With love,
Beverly
Theodore Roosevelt School
Compton, Calif.

1952

Dear Lau

How

Your ___ very much. Our
teacher is ___ he has already read
us "The ___ n Creek," and By
the Shor

Our ___ ols that you went
too. On ___ rings, and we have
a grove. ___ r-square, kickball,
baseball, and netball.

In our room we have two big blackboards and five bulletin-boards.
We have a piano. We have 39 children in our room.

We wrote some poems. Here is my poem.

There was a little girl named Mary
    Whose sisters were Laura, Grace, and Carrie
They lived in a log house by Plum Creek.
    They loved to play hide and seek.

With love from all the class,
Sincerely,
Margaret
Theodore Roosevelt School
Compton, Calif.

at the Theodore

11/22/09

She hau
   name was Jack.
Oh how Laura and Mary likeu
   to Play
One day they tumbled down
   in the hay.

                              La Juana

Laura and Mary
When Laura's family moved to
their house at first they only
had a cloth door.
But as each of the days passed by
they built on a little more.

   Jack their dog, liked to play
With Laura and Mary day by day.

They were always thankful
for what they got
　　They had awful nice neighbors
one was Mr. Scott.

                                        Judy

My Poem
Yesterday the rain fell in great big
　　drops,
The farmers know that it will help
　　their crops.
To day it is sunny and I went
　　out to play,
And I saw lots of interesting things
　　to day.

I saw some corn, grapes, orange trees,
　　and other things,
Boys were flying their kites with
　　long, long, strings.

                                        by Pauline

My Poem

Some pioneers were
   moving west,
Looking for the land
   they liked best.
Slowly moving over
   the plains,
Through dirt, storms
   and rains,
Over the great mountains
   and hills,
Through the land
   with many thrills,
They felt at last an
   ocean breeze,
And smelled blossoms
   of the orange trees.

                           Wanda

March 14, 1952

Dear Laura,

Sunshine brings flowers and flowers bring writing, and writing always brings good friends. I am writing to you because I liked all your books, especially <u>These Happy Golden Years</u>.

You have only six in the family but we have eleven, Marilyn who is 17, March 9, Frank 15, Joyce 14, I am 12, Philip 11, Carol Ann 8, Freddy 7, Kenneth 5. Leon is going to be one year old March 27.

I am in the seventh grade. I will have to go to school here only one more year because we have only eight grades in this school. We are building a new school here in Petersburg. Our old one, which we are still going to school in is pretty worn out. Its steps have round holes in from so many children always going up and down the steps. We don't have hot lunches in school, so we all have to bring dinner buckets.

I liked reading all your books so much that I read them over three times each. Or even more times. Please send me a picture of you. May God bless you Laura.

Your Petersburg friend,
Iva Mae
St. Peter & Paul School
Petersburg, Iowa

March 15, 1952

Dearest Laura,

    My name is Jeannie. I am 12 years old and in 7th grade.

    How old is your daughter Rose? Is she still living? How old is she? Do you have any other children?

    Are Ida and Elmer still living? What are their children's names? Where do they live?

    Did you teach school after you were married?

    How long did you and Almanzo live in South Dakota before you moved to Missouri?

    I was very sorry to hear about Almanzo and Pa and Ma and Grace, Carrie and Mary passing away.

    How old did Pa and Ma and Grace, Carrie and Mary live to be?

    I have read all eight of the books you have written and enjoyed them very much. I read most of my time. Sometimes even when I'm supposed to be studying Calif. Hist. and Geography. Mother say's that I read to much and am a "Book worm".

    I have one sister that is almost 2 years younger than I. Her name is Peggy. We have a gray and white cat named

Smokey. He is real big and awful pretty.

I don't suppose I'll ever find out the answers to all these questions I have asked you, but I can always hope that you will have time to write a few lines to me.

Sincerely yours,
Jeannie
Lindsay, Calif.

P.S. Please write if you have time.

March 19, 1952

Dear Mrs. Wilder,

We have been reading your books and we love them so much. I am only in the second grade but my! I enjoy hearing our teacher read your books. We are reading The Long Winter. We wish you could come to visit us. We have a very nice school.

Love to you,
Deanna Lynn
Spirit Lake, Iowa

March 21, 1952

Dear Mrs. Wilder,

I hope you are well.

I like best of all "Little House In The Big Woods,"
"These Happy Golden Years," "Farmer Boy," and "The
Long Winter." I like them so well that I bought a series
for myself. I earned the money picking beans on hot
August days. When I get started I can't hardly stop. I
have hardly ever read better books. I have been at lake
Pepin.

I wondered what became of Mary, Carrie and Grace.

A Wisc. farm boy,
Paul
Mondovi, Wisc.

March 28, 1952

Dear Mrs. Wilder,

We have just finished reading your series of books and have liked them very, very much. Mrs. Dawson, our teacher, read the books to us last year and we liked them so much we had her read them again this year.

We would like to know if any of your sisters or Almanzo is still living?

How did it happen that you decided to write the story of your life? Was it because Mary would have liked to and couldn't? We think that it was nice the way you helped her get to go to college.

We surely can sympathize with you having a sister that was blind as we are attending a Physically Handicapped room. The two of us that are writing this letter have had polio. When Mrs. Dawson first started this room she had six children in it. Now there are twelve of us.

We have been anxious to know about some of the things in the story you didn't mention. If you have time would you answer some of our questions, please?

How old were you when you first started writing your books? Did your father and mother live on the claim five years? How long were they on it after that? How long did you and Almanzo live in your little house in the woods? How many of your sisters got married? Did you or your sisters have any children? How long did you keep those pretty horses, Prince and Lady? Did you ever teach school after you were married? What did Almanzo's mother and sister say when they found out you got married before they got there? Did you ever hear anymore from Nellie Oleson after you got married? We are glad that Almanzo married you and not Nellie. Did any of your girl friends you wrote about marry the boys they were going with in the story? Did Royal Wilder ever get married? Did you travel any farther west after you were married?

After Mrs. Dawson got through reading the books to us we wanted to know if you were still living. We asked our city librarian and she gave us your address.

Yours truly,
Marlene
Juanita
Room 4,
Washington
School
Council Bluffs,
Iowa

Laura made these notes on the back of Marlene and Juanita's envelope to remind herself what to write in her reply.

April 8, 1952

Dearest Mrs. Wilder,

Ever since the day I got your letter, I have been trying to think just what I would say to you in the letter I have been planning to write for so long. I still couldn't think of what to write so I'll just say what comes into my mind. It is absolutely impossible to tell you how I have enjoyed the books that you wrote about the life of you and your dear family. You might be interested in knowing that I am saving 50¢ out of my allowance each week for buying the entire series of Laura Ingalls Wilder books. I want them to give my children and grandchildren as much enjoyment as they have given me. Being the editor of our school paper I have a special interest in reading and writing. But I know I would treasure each of your stories just as much anyway. I appreciated the information you sent about your parents and sisters and friends very much. I am terribly sorry that none of them are still living but I thank God that you are still happy on your farm in Missouri.

I will tell you a little about my family and myself.

I am fifteen years old. My birthday is January 8th. I have two wonderful parents, and my mother is very beautiful. She has dark brown hair and eyes of the same color. As she is only 5'2", I tease her about being so short. <u>I love her</u>

very <u>much</u>. Daddy is just as swell. I have a sweet little rascal of a brother. He is 11 yrs. old. Tom will be 12 May 8th. Doesn't that sound like a wonderful family? It is! In case you wonder what I look like, my hair is light brown, I have hazel eyes, I am 5'4½" tall, and I weigh 110 pounds. We have a sweet black cocker-spaniel dog. Her name is Duchess and she is about nine years old.

We live in a beautiful white colonial style home with green shutters. We have a large lawn which contains 33 trees. There is a park and swimming pool just beyond the houses across the street from us. We moved to this home 2 years ago last month. We are very happy here.

My aunt, uncle, & cousins—Judy, Diann, and Joann are coming for Easter vacation. We always have lots of fun together. I'm so excited.

If you have any time I would love to have a note from you. However, don't feel that you need to write me.

I hope you have a Happy Easter. God bless you dear Mrs. Wilder!

Love,
Sue
Des Moines, Iowa

April 29, 1952

Dear Mrs. Wilder,

    We enjoyed your books about you and your family. The teacher read all the books except one. We enjoy them very much. We were glad to get the letter. I missed school that day when the letter came. We like Mrs. Hort to read the stories about you. We do many things in our room. We do word work. We paint and we sew. We do cooking. We make candy and cake jello and cut cake and lots of other kinds of food in our Special Training Class. We are going to have an Open House Night. Tuesday April 29, 1952. We are going to display the best work that we did in our room. I hope you will get well soon. Is Mary alive? I hope she is. We will like the book that Mrs. Hort is reading to us now. It is The Little House in the Big Woods.

Your friend,
Gilbert
River Boulevard School
Bakersfield, Calif.

In June 1953, the fifth grade of the Theodore Roosevelt School in Compton, California, sent a leather autograph album to Laura. Inside the album each student had written a personal note to Laura telling her what his or her favorite Little House episode or book was. On the flyleaf, the students wrote:

To Mrs. Laura Ingalls Wilder with sincere gratitude
from Grade 5
    Room 8
    T. Roosevelt School
    Compton, California

The following are a few selections from the album:
Do you remember when Ma and Pa gave you the Autograph Album? I hope you still have it, but if you don't have it we are sending you one.

Kenneth

I love your books very much. I think the best book is On the Banks of Plum Creek. I wish you would write more books. Do you remember Nellie Oleson? She is a big showoff. Oh, I love your books!

Love,
Marilyn

Laura, brown curls are just as pretty as blond curls. Did you have fun playing with the pig's tail? I love your books very much. I wish you would write more books. Thank you.

Sandra

I wish that your books could be put into pictures so that more people could see your stories on television so they could see your hardships, laughter and sorrows.

> Sincerely,
> James

We enjoy your books every day after we come in from noon Play. Through Rain or shine we read them all the time with memories of you and your family.

> Love always,
> Patricia Ann

Here is a poem I made of your story:
> You have had
> a rugged life
> and now that you
> are a wife
> I want to thank
> you for your story
> of the days of Mary and Laurey.

> From
> Hubert

I like the place where you walked a half a mile to teach five children and stayed with the Brewster's.

> Love,
> Sharon

November 19, 1954

Dear Mrs. Wilder,

   I love to read, and I have read all your books. I am
10½ and in the fifth grade. There is one sentence that I
like best in all your books, "Laura sat on the seat and
thought complaints to her-self." I too am going to be a
teacher. If you can would you please send me a picture
of your-self, and a signature.

                                    love,
                                    Betsy
                                    Junction City, Ore.
P.S. Just tonight I read a chapter of the Little House In
the big Woods to my brother Johnny.

November 30, 1956

Dear Laura Ingalls Wilder,

This is "Book Week" so we want to write you a letter. We love your books so much. They are wonderful. Are you writing a new book now? We hope you are. We have almost all of your books in our library at school. You are so much like we girls would like to be.

We would like so much to have you write us a letter. Do you ever send a picture of yourself to anyone? We would enjoy having your picture in our room. We will publish your letter in our "Little Red School House" so all of the children can read it, unless you tell us not to. The Little Red School House is a newspaper that our room puts out. All of the children in town write for it and our city daily paper prints it in one of its regular issues every two weeks. We are sending you a copy of it so that you can see what it is like.

Thank you for writing such good stories for us. We love you. We hope you will write many more.

Your friends,
The Fourth Grade
Roosevelt School
Arkansas City, Kans.
By: Connie
    Carol
    Phillip
    Bob

February 4, 1957

Dear Mrs. Wilder,

We are enjoying your books so very much and we are learning a lot from them too about the way people used to live. Not many people would think of writing about their adventures or things of that sort, and I think it was nice of you to write about yourself so that other people could enjoy your adventures. I hope you have a happy birthday and a lot more wonderful ones to come.

Yours truly,
Scott
Riverside, Calif.

February 4, 1957

Dear Mrs. Laura Ingalls Wilder,

How are you? We are fine. We enjoy your story of ON THE BANKS OF PLUM CREEK. Our Teacher is Mrs. Temple. We are in the 4th grade. Our Teacher is reading On The Banks of Plum Creek to us at school. She is going to read By the Shores of Silver Lake. How is every-one. Will you write to us. We will write again. Mrs. Temple is senting you a Birthday card with all of our names on it. If you write to me I'll take your letter to school and read it to all the children.

Yours Truly,
Jackie
Joann
Pendleton, Ore.

February 5, 1957

Dear Mrs. Wilder,

I can't tell you how much I have loved your books. I think your right there reading your books to me.

Ann and I went to the library to see when you were born. When we found out it was a day after Ann's we decided to send you a birthday card. We thought we might make your gingerbread for the fourth grade class. I hope you have many more birthdays after this one.

Cordially yours,
Patricia Lou
Columbus, Ohio

February 5, 1957

Dear Laura,

I hope I am not insulting you by calling you by your first name, only you seem such a close friend since I have read all your books.

I certainly hope you have a happy birthday because you surely deserve it and you are such a nice lady and Pat and I really do admire you.

Cordially,
Ann
Columbus, Ohio

February 7, 1957

Dear Laura Ingalls Wilder,

I enjoy the books that you have wrote very much. I don't know which book I like best. I just couldn't believe that all those adventures you had were true until I read them my self.

My grandma lives close to De Smet where you once lived and wrote about. My grandma is 84 years old. Once when she was a little girl her father stopped to rest one night at the home of Frank and Ezra Ingals. My grandma also has told me the story of the 1880 blizzard. She was little girl then and her name was Myrta Adams.

My name is Myrta and I have read all of your books. I wish you were writing another.

In De Smet they give plays about your books, every summer.

I found your address in the paper and so I thought I would send you a letter telling how much I like your books. Mother is going to try to get me all of your books for me to keep.

I live in Mt. Lake, Minnesota. My Grandma's home is in South Dakota in Erwin. Erwin wa built on my great grandfather's homestead. He had a store there when the town first started. My grandma is living with us this winter. Your books are the best I have ever read.

I am in 5 grade and like school. It is a lot easier to go now than it was when you were little. I am 10 years old.

Sincerely Yours,
Myrta
Mt. Lake, Minn.

February 7, 1957

Dear Mrs. Wilder,

 May this friendly birthday wish that comes to you today bring much happiness.

 I like to read books. My favorite story of yours is On the Bank of Plum Creek. May Laughter and cheer come to you throughout the coming years.

Your Friend,
Theresa
Hoyt School
Saginaw, Mich.

February 7, 1957

Dear Mrs. Wilder,

 I go to Hoyt School in Saginaw Mich. And my teacher's name is Miss Stineman. And I am in the fifth grade room 203. I am ten myself. And I read a lot of books. But you are my favorite writer. I have read a good many stories of yours and they are very good. I have five of your books and there are some books at school. I think the Little House in the Big Woods is the most exciting of all your stories. I wish you a very happy birthday and all the luck in the world.

Your friend,
Floyd
Hoyt School
Saginaw, Mich.

February 7, 1957

Dear Miss Wilder,

I wish you a very happy birthday. I wish you get lots
of presents to day. I am sending you this letter to tell you
how I enjoy your books. I read The "Little House in the
Big Woods." I like the part when their father scared the
two little and when he was singing Yankee Doodle.

I am in the 5th grade and I am ten years old. We did
free hand maps on Michigan. We have a book you wrote.
It is called "The Farmer Boy." I haven't read it but I am
pretty soon. Today is my grandmother's birthday too and
my sister is going to make her a cake.

I learned to write like this last year. My name is
Rosalinda. I was in group two reading and now I am in
reading one. We are finishing the Reader's Digest. We
are going to get new books pretty soon. I am in group
one in arithmetic.

Your friend,
Rosalinda
Hoyt School
Saginaw, Mich.

February 7, 1957

Dear Mrs. Wilder,

    I am Tim in fifth grade, and I'm wishing you a very happy birthday for this year and a happy one for everyone you have.

    I've been reading your books for a long time and the one I liked the best was "On The Banks Of Plum Creek."

    When I was in the third grade at the other school Mrs. Sitze let us put on a play of one of your books. It was the one about the prairie fire. In that play I played "Pa."

                 Your friend,
                 Tim
                 Hoyt School
                 Saginaw, Mich.

February 7, 1957

Dear Mrs. Wilder,

I know that today is your birthday so I want to wish you a <u>very</u> HAPPY BIRTHDAY. My name is Nancy & as you can see I go to Hoyt School. My age is ten (10). "By the Banks of Plum Creek" is my favorite book of yours.

Getting back to myself, I have two (2) fish named Comet & Star, I also have a turtle named Scoots. My favorite subject at school is Spelling. I read a lot but I like <u>thick</u> books & not skinny ones. I just love hard written books. I'll have to say Good Bye, with the best of luck & health.

Love,
Nancy
Hoyt School
Saginaw, Mich.

February 7, 1957

Dear Mrs. Wilder,

I hope you are feeling fine and I want to wish you a very happy birthday and many more of them too.

I have a mother, father, sister, and brother and a dog named Queeny. Have you any pets?

I'm in the fifth grade at Hoyt school. My favorite subjects are arithmetic, spelling and geography.

Have you any hobbies? I do. I collect china ware, story book dolls, stamps, cups, and many other things.

I have read the book of "On the Banks of Plum Creek." I enjoyed it very much it is one of my favorite books.

Again I will say "Happy Birthday and best wishes."

Lovingly,
Frances
Hoyt School
Saginaw, Mich.

February 7, 1957

Dear Mrs. Wilder,

    I wish you a happy, happy birthday.

    Do you have any pets? I have a bird named Paddy & she talks; it's a girl but she says "Pretty boy, What are doing" & she shakes her head yes.

    I've one sister & one brother, two nephews, a brother in law and I'm going to have a sister in law pretty soon.

    I am interested in insects are you? Up north this summer I caught grasshoppers, dragonflies, caterpillars & many others. I also caught frogs and turtles. I had a painted turtle named Cocao.

    I wish you many more happy birthdays.

                    Love,
                    Karen
                    Hoyt School
                    Saginaw, Mich.

Laura at home on Rocky Ridge Farm, 1954

In 1947, a department store in Chicago held a birthday party in Laura's honor. Laura and Almanzo were invited to attend the party, and Laura was also invited to appear as a guest on "The Hobby Horse," a popular radio program for children. Laura could not attend the party or the radio program. To make sure that the children who invited her would not be too disappointed, though, she mailed 200 autographs to the store and wrote a long letter telling them all about her life since the Little House books. This letter answered many of the questions that were most frequently asked by Laura's fans.

In the 1950's, the rheumatism in Laura's hands made it too painful for her to continue answering each fan letter by hand. So Laura and her publisher, Harper Brothers, put together a composite letter based on several letters Laura had written over the years, including the one she sent to the children in Chicago. This is the letter that was sent to every fan who wrote Laura:

Dear Children:

I was born in the "Little House in the Big Woods" of Wisconsin on February 7 in the year of 1867. I lived everything that happened in my books. It is a long story, filled with sunshine and shadow. . . .

After our marriage Almanzo and I lived for a little while in the little gray house on the tree claim. In the year 1894 we and our little daughter, Rose, left Dakota in a covered wagon and moved to a farm in the Ozarks. We cleared the land and built our own farmhouse. Eventually we had 200 acres of improved land, a herd of cows, good hogs, and the best laying flock of hens in the country. For many years we did all our own work, but now almost all of the land has been rented or sold. For recreation we used to ride horseback or in our buggy—later on, our Chrysler. We read and played music and attended church socials. In 1949 Almanzo died at the age of 92. We had been married for 63 years.

You may be interested to know what happened to some of the other people you met in my books. Ma and Pa lived for a while on their homestead and then moved into town, where Pa did carpentry. After Mary graduated from the College for the Blind, she lived at home. She was always cheerful and busy with her work, her books, and music. Carrie worked for *The De Smet News* for a while after finishing high school, and then she married a mine owner and moved to the Black Hills. Grace married a farmer and lived a few miles outside of De Smet. All of them have been dead for some years now.

Mary Power married the young banker and did not live many years. Ida married her Elmer and moved to California. Cap Garland was killed in the explosion of a threshing machine engine. Nellie Oleson went East, married, and moved to Louisiana, where she is now buried.

Several years before Almanzo's death, he and I took a trip

back to De Smet for a reunion with our old friends. Many of the old buildings had been replaced. Everywhere we went, we recognized faces, but we were always surprised to find them old and gray like ourselves, instead of being young as in our memories. There is one thing that will always remain the same to remind people of little Laura's days on the prairie, and that is Pa's fiddle.

The Little House books are stories of long ago. Today our way of living and our schools are much different; so many things have made living and learning easier. But the real things haven't changed. It is still best to be honest and truthful; to make the most of what we have; to be happy with simple pleasures and to be cheerful and have courage when things go wrong. Great improvements in living have been made because every American has always been free to pursue his happiness, and so long as Americans are free, they will continue to make our country ever more wonderful.

With love to you all and best wishes for your happiness, I am Sincerely, your friend,

Laura Ingalls Wilder

There are many Little House sites and museums that you can visit to see where Laura actually lived. Some sites and museums will send you newsletters that contain information about the site and about Laura. Always remember to include a self-addressed stamped envelope when you write!

For information about the Little House in the Big Woods site and the Laura Ingalls Wilder newsletter, write to:
> The Laura Ingalls Wilder Memorial Society, Inc.
> P.O. Box 269
> Pepin, WI 54759

For information about the Little House on the Prairie site, write to:
> Little House on the Prairie, Inc.
> P.O. Box 110
> Independence, KS 67301

For information about the Plum Creek site, write to:
> The Laura Ingalls Wilder Museum
> 330 Eighth Street
> P.O. Box 58J
> Walnut Grove, MN 56180

For information about the De Smet sites and newsletter, write to:
> Laura Ingalls Wilder Memorial Society
> Box 344
> De Smet, SD 57231

For information about the Rocky Ridge site and newsletter, write to:
> Laura Ingalls Wilder–Rose Wilder Lane Home Association
> Rt. 1, Box 24
> Mansfield, MO 65704

For information about the Farmer Boy site and newsletter, write to:
> Almanzo and Laura Ingalls Wilder Association
> Box 283
> Malone, NY 12953